Looking at . . . Oviraptor
A Dinosaur from the CRETACEOUS Period

**For a free color catalog describing Gareth Stevens' list of high-quality books,
call 1-800-542-2595 (USA) or 1-800-461-9120 (Canada).
Gareth Stevens' Fax: (414) 225-0377.**

Library of Congress Cataloging-in-Publication Data available upon request from publisher.
Fax: (414) 225-0377 for the attention of the Publishing Records Department.

ISBN 0-8368-1347-2

This North American edition first published in 1995 by
Gareth Stevens Publishing
1555 North RiverCenter Drive, Suite 201
Milwaukee, Wisconsin 53212 USA

This U.S. edition © 1995 by Gareth Stevens, Inc. Created with original © 1995 by Quartz
Editorial Services, Premier House, 112 Station Road, Edgware HA8 7AQ U.K.

Consultant: Dr. David Norman, Director of the Sedgwick Museum of Geology,
University of Cambridge, England.

Additional artwork by Clare Herronneau.

Printed in the United States of America

1 2 3 4 5 6 7 8 9 99 98 97 96 95

Looking at . . . Oviraptor

A Dinosaur from the CRETACEOUS Period

by Tamara Green

Illustrated by Tony Gibbons

THE NEW
DINOSAUR
COLLECTION

Gareth Stevens Publishing
MILWAUKEE

Contents

Introducing
Oviraptor

Some dinosaurs were fierce carnivores, always on the lookout for victims to devour and bones to gnaw. Others were herbivores, eating only plants, leaves, twigs, and berries, but no meat. But for many years now, scientists have thought that one dinosaur in particular had a strange appetite for raw eggs. That was **Oviraptor** (OVE-IH-RAP-TOR).

So how did this odd-looking dinosaur spend its day? And how did its bizarre appetite for eggs develop?

Read on and learn more about this fascinating creature. Scientists now have quite a bit of information concerning the world of **Oviraptor**.

They have even found, as you will discover, an **Oviraptor** egg, with a developing baby dinosaur inside it! As a result, lots of old ideas about **Oviraptor** may perhaps be about to change.

5

Ugly brute

Perhaps you enjoy eggs for breakfast. If so, you have something in common with **Oviraptor** — although you probably like yours cooked, and not raw!

Oviraptor lived about 80 million years ago.

Its remains were first discovered in Mongolia, in Asia. They were found by an American paleontologist named George Olsen during an expedition in 1923. One of the first things scientists realized was that **Oviraptor** seemed to have had two prongs in the roof of its mouth instead of teeth.

Scientists believe a fully-grown **Oviraptor** was 6.5 feet (2 meters) long, and only about as tall as you are. Looking very birdlike, it was quick on its feet and probably ran on its two slim back legs, using clawed, three-fingered hands for grabbing things. **Oviraptor** had to be nimble because it needed to make a quick

You might think it would be easy to identify **Oviraptor** by its very strange head. But, as you will soon discover, the size and shape of the bulbous nose bump varied quite a bit from one **Oviraptor** to another. So not all of them looked exactly the same.

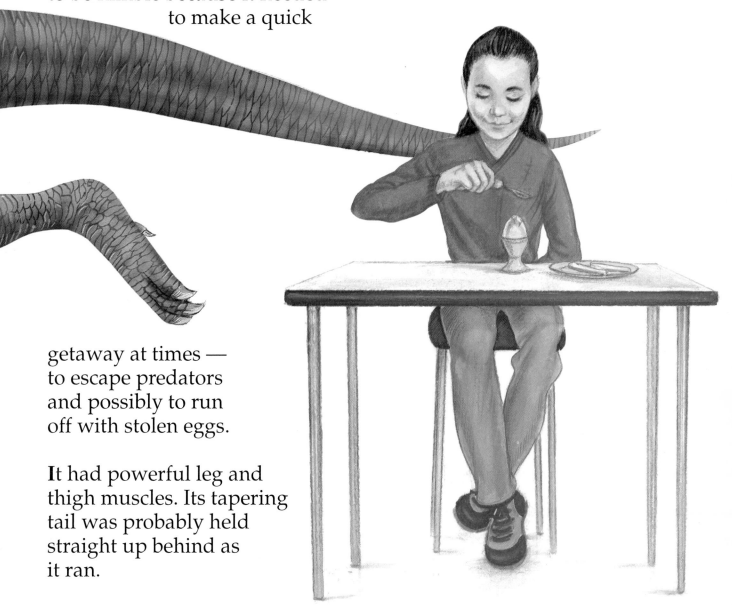

getaway at times — to escape predators and possibly to run off with stolen eggs.

It had powerful leg and thigh muscles. Its tapering tail was probably held straight up behind as it ran.

Unusual skeleton

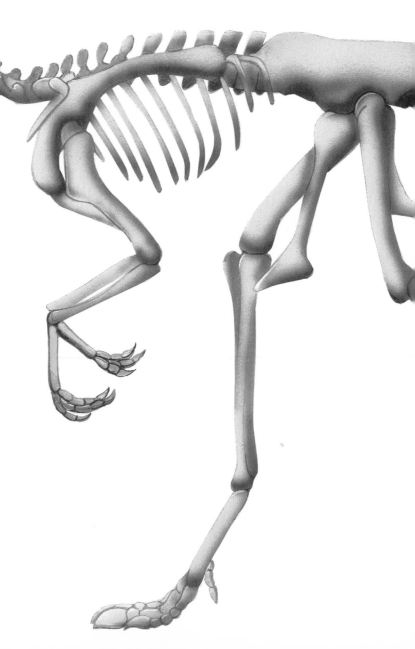

The first remains of **Oviraptor** to be dug up in Mongolia included just part of the neck and a few ribs, as well as shoulder bones, a left fore-limb, and most of a right hand.

Since then, better skeletons have been discovered, however. All show that **Oviraptor** was quite unusual for a dinosaur in two particular ways.

First of all, it had a collarbone in its shoulder that was shaped much like the wishbone that is sometimes pulled for good luck from a whole, cooked chicken.

Previously, scientists believed no dinosaurs at all had a *single* bone in the shoulder like this.

Instead, they thought dinosaurs always had a *pair* of shoulder bones. So leading paleontologists were quite surprised by this discovery. They were astonished, too, when they realized that not all **Oviraptor** heads were the same.

So the skulls that have been dug up are not all exactly like the one shown in this skeletal reconstruction.

Some had a nose bump like this one; but others had more of a crest on their heads, as you will find out later in this book.

Nevertheless, the heads all seem to have had strong, toothless jaws covered in horn.

Oviraptor's skeleton was slim and light — all the better for making a quick escape when it needed to.

Its three clawed fingers on each hand were long and flexible, with the first finger a little shorter than the other two. It was used in much the same way as we use our thumbs today, to help grasp things.

Without this shorter finger, this egg thief might never have managed to hold anything round and slippery — like an egg!

Notice how **Oviraptor**'s tail tapered, getting thinner toward a point at the end. And take a look at its three main toes that ended in sharp claws. Like many other dinosaurs, **Oviraptor** also had an extra tiny, toelike growth, as you can see.

Mongolian

It is not hard to understand why **Oviraptor** was given a name that means "egg thief." Quite simply, at the time it was named, scientists thought they had proof to show that it stole other dinosaurs' eggs and then feasted on them.

During their expedition to Mongolia in the 1920s, scientists found the flattened skull and also the skeleton of a lightly built predator.

These bones were on top of what they thought was a nest of eggs belonging to another dinosaur, a **Protoceratops** (PRO-TOE-SER-A-TOPS).

Curiously, the jaws of the predator appeared to have been toothless, but the scientists noticed there were signs of a beak that must have been a little like that of today's turtles.

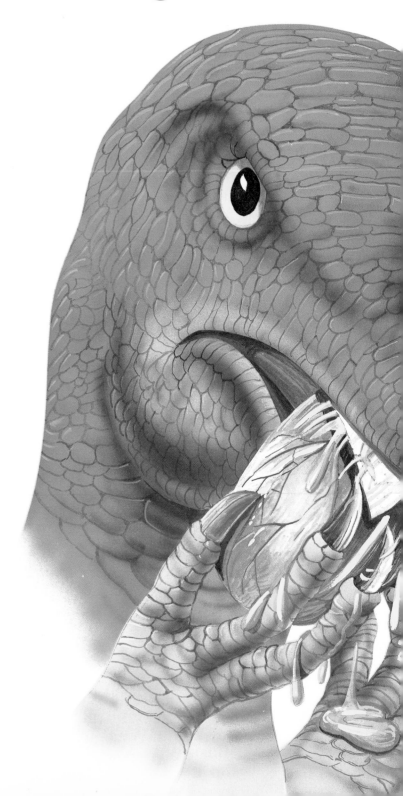

egg thief

Eggs, the scientists thought, would have been an ideal food for a dinosaur with no true teeth in its jaws. That horny beak would have been good, too, for cracking open eggshells. But that was not all they discovered.

It was soon found that there were two bony prongs in the roof of **Oviraptor**'s mouth. These would also have been suited to crushing shells of all kinds. And the large lower jaw could have exerted a lot of pressure on anything with a tough outer coating – eggs, for instance.

Oviraptor's claws were also well adapted to holding something that was oval in shape, and perhaps warm and slippery.

So it seemed likely that the **Oviraptor** whose remains were found over that nest might have been crushed to death by a furious **Protoceratops** parent as it tried to protect its clutch of eggs.

Other scientists believe the **Oviraptor** may have been stifled to death by a sandstorm, just as it was on the point of stealing an egg.

Or maybe its heart simply gave out at that moment because it was old for a dinosaur, or perhaps ill. Then again, some other predator might have fought with the **Oviraptor** over the nest and won the battle.

We may never know for sure. But it is fascinating to try to guess what might actually have happened that Cretaceous day, all those millions of years ago.

Different heads,

Take a good look at the two heads illustrated here. The one on the left looks just like the **Oviraptor** you will find on the other pages in this book. The head on the right, however, is quite different.

As you can see, instead of the nose bump, there is a large crest that rises over the top of most of the head on the right.

In fact, both are **Oviraptor** heads. According to what scientists have so far discovered, not all **Oviraptor** had the same type of head. No one knows why this might have been, but we can guess.

same creature

Or perhaps only the males had these large head crests in order to impress the females. Maybe the larger a male's crest, the more powerful and attractive the animal was.

There could be several possibilities. Which do *you* think is the most likely?

Perhaps the larger head crest only occurred in an adult **Oviraptor**. Maybe the crest was useful for pushing thick vegetation that was in the way.

The two heads shown here have been colored by our artist in two shades to make the differences in their shapes as clear as possible. But no one, not even the experts, knows for sure what color the skin of any of the dinosaurs was.

13

Greedy omnivore

The day had just dawned and **Oviraptor** was starving. It had not had a meal since the previous evening. An omnivore, it ate both flesh and vegetation. But it also had an appetite for eggs — dinosaur eggs — and always kept an eye out for a tempting clutch of them.

It was **Oviraptor**'s lucky day. What a treat for breakfast!

It had spied a dinosaur nest behind some nearby bushes. There were several newly laid eggs in it. The mother and other family members did not seem to be anywhere nearby.

Oviraptor looked quickly around, and then crept toward the nest full of eggs that had been dug in sandy ground.

Greedily, **Oviraptor** grabbed at the nearest egg. Maybe it would have time to have more than just a snack and crack open several of them.

Just as it grabbed one egg, however, a threatening growl broke the silence of the early morning.

The mother, a **Protoceratops**, had gone off to feed, leaving her nest unprotected for a while.

Her beak was sharp and cut easily through the **Oviraptor**'s flesh.

Ouch! The **Oviraptor** screamed in pain as its tail began to bleed. It dropped the stolen egg, which smashed on the ground.

The **Oviraptor** suddenly was not nearly so brave. It felt unable to defend itself against this attack.

Speedily, the thief ran off. Breakfast would have to consist of

She now returned to find it being raided. Violently angry, the mother shook her frill at the **Oviraptor** before taking one great bite at its tail, then another.

something else. Eggs were most definitely not on the menu that morning.

Amazing new

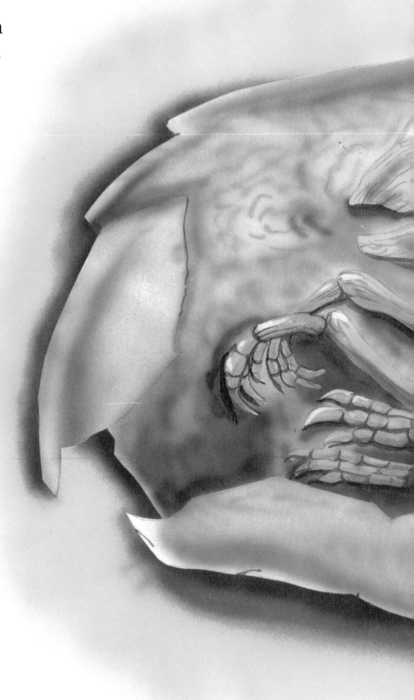

In November 1994, scientists from the American Museum of Natural History and the Mongolian Academy of Sciences had a very exciting joint announcement to make to the world about a recent discovery.

They had found a dinosaur egg, approximately 80 million years old, at a site in Ukhaa Tolgod, in Mongolia. In it were the remains of a developing baby dinosaur, curled up with its head tucked near its knees. It must have been almost ready to hatch when it died, because it was quite large. But no one knows why it was never born.

When whole, the egg probably measured 6 inches (15 centimeters) long and 2 inches (5 cm) wide. But when scientists found the egg, some of it had been weathered away. This meant they could see inside the egg without having to x-ray it.

egg discovery!

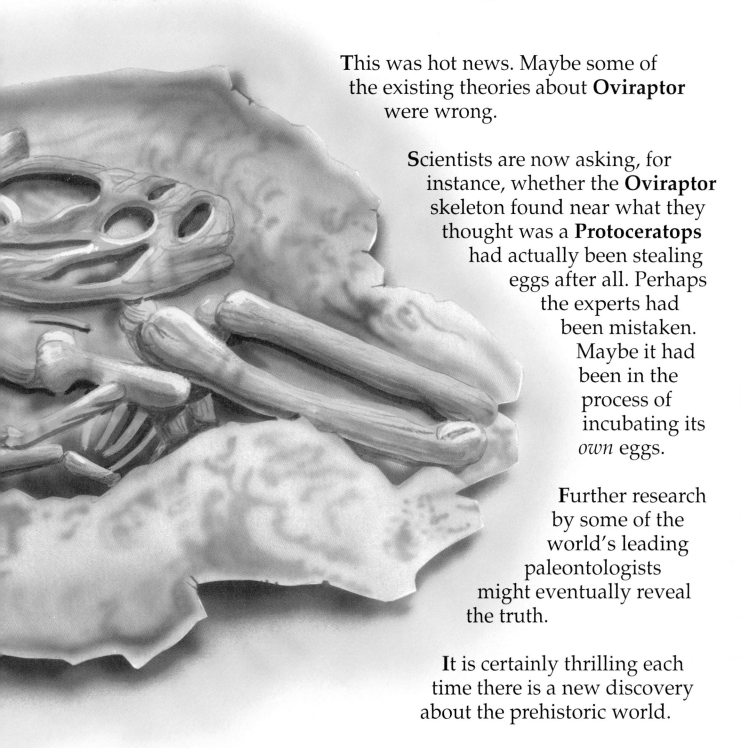

This was hot news. Maybe some of the existing theories about **Oviraptor** were wrong.

Scientists are now asking, for instance, whether the **Oviraptor** skeleton found near what they thought was a **Protoceratops** had actually been stealing eggs after all. Perhaps the experts had been mistaken. Maybe it had been in the process of incubating its *own* eggs.

Further research by some of the world's leading paleontologists might eventually reveal the truth.

It is certainly thrilling each time there is a new discovery about the prehistoric world.

Eighty million

Many of the dinosaurs that roamed the Mongolian landscape some 80 million years ago were peaceful herbivores that spent almost all of their time browsing on plant life for food.

Frilled **Protoceratops** was one of these herbivores and can be seen in the background here. **Avimimus** (AVE-EE-MIME-US) was another. It was small and very birdlike in appearance as its name, meaning "bird mimic," suggests. **Avimimus** had a toothless beak, long neck and tail, and perhaps also feather-covered, winglike arms. Scientists believe, though, that it could not fly.

Herbivores such as these constantly had to be on the lookout for fearsome predators such as **Tarbosaurus** (TAR-BO-SAW-RUS), a large flesh-eater with huge jaws and fangs.

Tarbosaurus probably needed to feed on the meat of at least two reasonably sized victims a day to survive.

Then, of course, there was also **Oviraptor**. As an omnivore, it ate raw meat as well as eggs and vegetation.

years ago

Although small by dinosaur standards, in this illustration **Oviraptor** looms large in the foreground as it savors the yolk of an egg it has stolen from the clutch in a nest. Giant **Tarbosaurus**, meanwhile, lurks in the distance, hankering for a feast of freshly killed **Oviraptor** meat.

Oviraptor data

Not all **Oviraptor**, as we have seen, had quite the same heads. But all had other features in common that have helped the experts identify **Oviraptor** remains.

Curved beak
Oviraptor used its horny beak to cut through flesh or vegetation. Its lower jaw was strong and curved, and helped it exert pressure on whatever it was taking in as food.

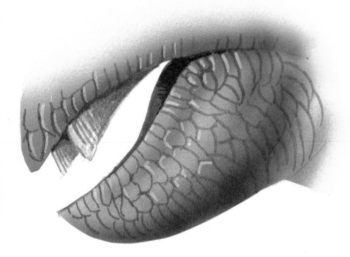

Piercing bite
Toothless, **Oviraptor** nevertheless had two prongs that were set in the roof of its mouth.

These prongs were sharp and pointed downward. They were great for biting into the hard surfaces of large fruits, nuts, and snails — and, of course, eggs.

Wishbone shoulder
Scientists soon noticed that **Oviraptor** had something quite special about its shoulder. This made it different from all other dinosaurs discovered so far. Instead of two bones, one on each side, there was just one curved bone, as if the usual two were somehow welded together. This collarbone, strange for a dinosaur, looked like a chicken wishbone.

It could use its shorter finger much like we use our thumbs, but to grip branches and grasp stolen eggs.

High-held tail

Oviraptor's tail was deep at the base and got slimmer toward the end. When it was standing still, its tail may have drooped. But when it ran, its tail was probably held out straight behind it, at body level, right off the ground, to help **Oviraptor** gain speed.

Clawed hands

Imagine that you had no thumbs. It would be difficult to grasp things, wouldn't it? **Oviraptor** was lucky: one of its three fingers was shorter than the other two.

Powerful legs

Look how muscular **Oviraptor**'s thighs and back legs were. It was very quick when it needed to escape a threatening predator or chase after some poor victim itself.

Other Mongolian dinosaurs

Mongolia is a country that lies in central Asia, between China and Russia. One-sixth the size of the United States, it covers an area of about 580,000 sq. miles (1.5 million sq. kilometers).

Let's now take a look at some of the other beasts whose remains have been dug up in dinosaur-rich graveyards there.

Many exciting dinosaur finds have been made in Mongolia, **Oviraptor** (1) among them.

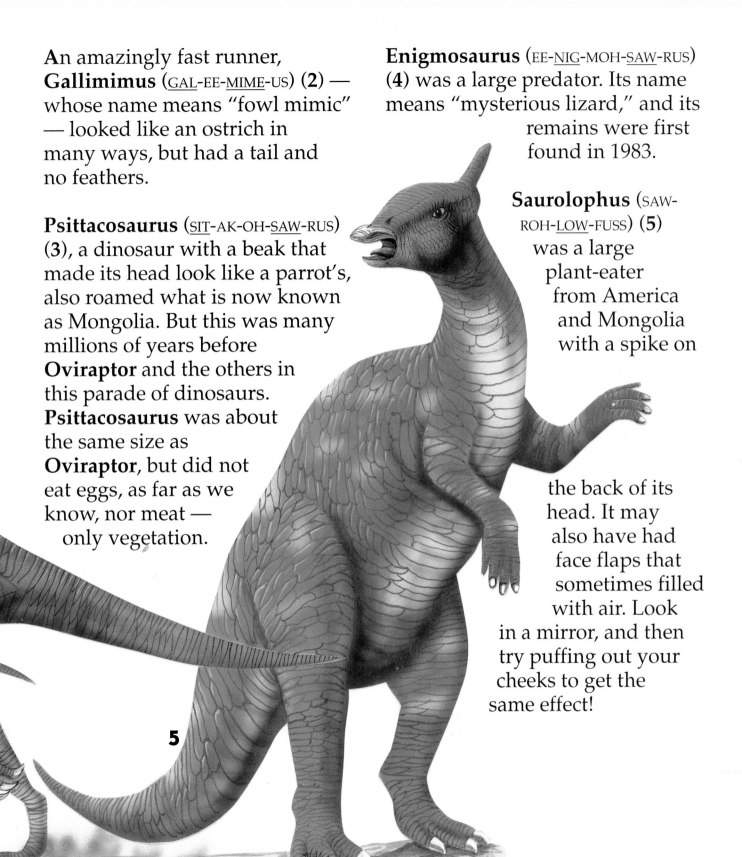

An amazingly fast runner, **Gallimimus** (<u>GAL</u>-EE-<u>MIME</u>-US) **(2)** — whose name means "fowl mimic" — looked like an ostrich in many ways, but had a tail and no feathers.

Psittacosaurus (<u>SIT</u>-AK-OH-<u>SAW</u>-RUS) **(3)**, a dinosaur with a beak that made its head look like a parrot's, also roamed what is now known as Mongolia. But this was many millions of years before **Oviraptor** and the others in this parade of dinosaurs. **Psittacosaurus** was about the same size as **Oviraptor**, but did not eat eggs, as far as we know, nor meat — only vegetation.

Enigmosaurus (EE-<u>NIG</u>-MOH-<u>SAW</u>-RUS) **(4)** was a large predator. Its name means "mysterious lizard," and its remains were first found in 1983.

Saurolophus (SAW-ROH-<u>LOW</u>-FUSS) **(5)** was a large plant-eater from America and Mongolia with a spike on the back of its head. It may also have had face flaps that sometimes filled with air. Look in a mirror, and then try puffing out your cheeks to get the same effect!

5

GLOSSARY

carnivores — meat-eating animals.

clutch — a nest of eggs; a group of persons, animals, or objects gathered together.

crest — a growth on top of an animal's head.

expedition — a journey or voyage.

herbivores — plant-eating animals.

omnivores — animals that eat both plants and other animals.

paleontologists — scientists who study the remains of plants and animals that lived millions of years ago.

predators — animals that kill other animals for food.

prongs — pointed tips or ends.

remains — a skeleton, bones, or dead body.

INDEX